FRED PICKER

6/22/79

For Bill
with Warm Regard,
Fred.

1. DUMMERSTON, VERMONT, 1979

FRED PICKER

AMERICAN
PHOTOGRAPHIC
BOOK PUBLISHING
COMPANY, INC.

Fred Picker is the author of "The Zone VI Work-shop," "The Fine Print," "Rapa Nui" (Easter Island) with Thor Heyerdahl, and "The Iceland Portfolio." He designs and markets photographic equipment, publishes a quarterly newsletter, directs a summer workshop program, and is a consultant to the Polaroid Corporation. He has been a trustee of The Friends of Photography and is a panel member of The Vermont Council on The Arts. His home is in Dummerston, Vermont.

For the constant encouragement and patient understanding that contributed to the making of these photographs and for her guidance in the selection and arrangement of them, I gratefully acknowledge the contribution of Lillian Farber to this book.

This book is published to accompany an exhibition at the Prakapas Gallery, New York, in June, 1979. The photographs were made between 1972 and 1979.

Design by Lance Hidy, Lancaster, N.H.
Typesetting by Monotype Composition Co., Boston
Printing by Thomas Todd Co., Boston
Binding by the New Hampshire Bindery, Concord
The paper is Warren's Lustro Offset Enamel

James Agee, "Let Us Now Praise Famous Men" reprinted by permission of Houghton Mifflin Company, copyright © renewed 1969 by Mia Fritsch Agee.

For in the immediate world, everything is to be discerned, for him who can discern it, and centrally and simply, without either dissection into science, or digestion into art, but with the whole of consciousness, seeking to perceive it as it stands: so that the aspect of a street in sunlight can roar in the heart of itself as a symphony, perhaps as no symphony can; and all of consciousness is shifted from the imagined, the revisive, to the effort to perceive simply the cruel radiance of what is.

James Agee
from *Let Us Now Praise Famous Men*

2. EGILSTADIR, ICELAND, 1975

3. VOGAR, ICELAND, 1975

4. GASPÉ, QUEBEC, 1977

5. HIGHGATE SPRINGS, VERMONT, 1976

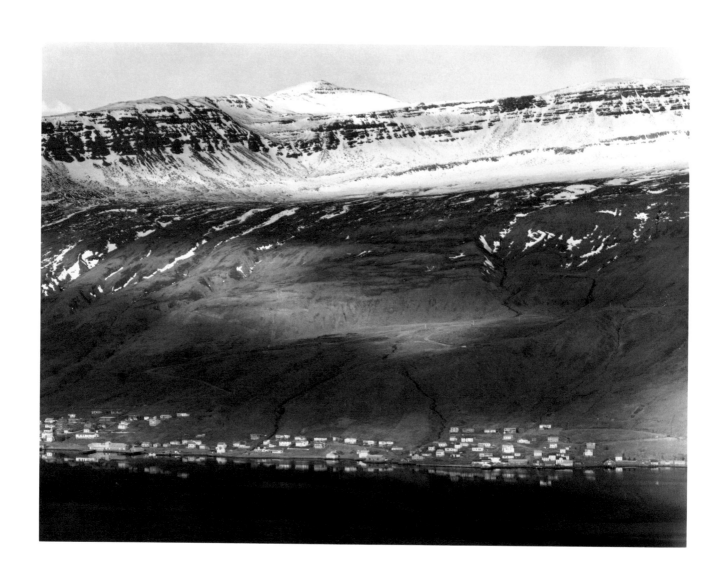

6. ESKIFJORDER, ICELAND, 1974

7. LISBON, NEW HAMPSHIRE, 1976

8. ROCKINGHAM, VERMONT, 1975

9. SOUTH WARDSBORO, VERMONT, 1976

10. EASTER ISLAND, 1973

11. EASTER ISLAND, 1973

12. RIPTON, VERMONT, 1976

13. GERDAR, ICELAND, 1974

14. NORTH PARIS, MAINE, 1976

15. LOWER GRANVILLE, VERMONT, 1978

16. NORTH THETFORD, VERMONT, 1977

17. WILLIAM CAPEN, ROCKINGHAM, VERMONT, 1975

18. PAMELA SOPER, PUTNEY, VERMONT, 1976

19. LEON STANLEY, VICTORY, VERMONT, 1975

20. DORRIT MERTON, WESTMINSTER WEST, VERMONT, 1976

21. ANN McBROOM, PUTNEY, VERMONT, 1976

22. PATRICIA NEAL, LONDON, 1978

23. GEORGE STANLEY, VICTORY, VERMONT, 1976

24. LEON TUKI HEI, EASTER ISLAND, 1973

25. MEGALITHIC TOMB, SLIGO, IRELAND, 1978

26. MOAI, EASTER ISLAND, 1973

27. MEGALITHIC TOMB, BALLYVAUGHAN, IRELAND, 1978

28. MYRDALSSANDER, ICELAND, 1975

29. WAITSFIELD, VERMONT, 1977

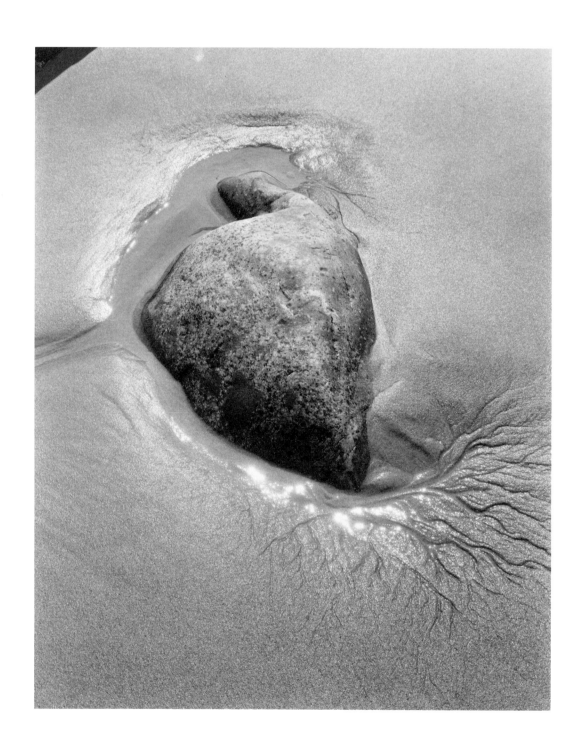

30. RHODE ISLAND, 1972

31. DUMMERSTON, VERMONT, 1977

32. WOODSTOCK, VERMONT, 1976

33. BAKER RIVER, NEW HAMPSHIRE, 1977

34. WESTMINSTER WEST, VERMONT, 1977

35. GRAFTON, VERMONT, 1977

36. SCHOODIC, MAINE, 1977

37. EAST PUTNEY BROOK, PUTNEY, VERMONT, 1977

38. GALE RIVER, FRANCONIA, NEW HAMPSHIRE, 1977

39. GROTON, VERMONT, 1979

40. DUMMERSTON, VERMONT, 1978

41. EAST ALSTEAD, NEW HAMPSHIRE, 1979

42. SKEIDERARJOKULL, ICELAND, 1975

43. SCHOODIC, MAINE, 1977

44. BURNT WOOD AND ICE, BELLOWS FALLS, VERMONT, 1975

45. PUTNEY, VERMONT, 1978

46. WESTMINSTER WEST, VERMONT, 1979

47. CALAIS, VERMONT, 1978

48. EAST BROOKFIELD, VERMONT, 1976

49. ADAMANT, VERMONT, 1978

50. STICKNEY BROOK, WEST DUMMERSTON, VERMONT, 1976

51. SECOND BRANCH, WHITE RIVER, EAST BETHEL, VERMONT, 1978

52. SCHOODIC, MAINE, 1977

53. HARTLAND FOUR CORNERS, VERMONT, 1977

54. MAINE COAST, 1977

55. MARLBORO, VERMONT, 1978

56. QUARRY, VERSHIRE, VERMONT, 1977

57. QUARRY, DORSET, VERMONT, 1977

58. PEACHAM, VERMONT, 1976

59. TOPSHAM, VERMONT, 1979

60. BAKER RIVER, NEW HAMPSHIRE, 1977

61. WHITE PLAINS, NEW YORK, 1972

62. DUMMERSTON, VERMONT, 1978

63. SCHOODIC, MAINE, 1977

64. DUMMERSTON, VERMONT, 1978

65. KLEIFERVATN, ICELAND, 1974

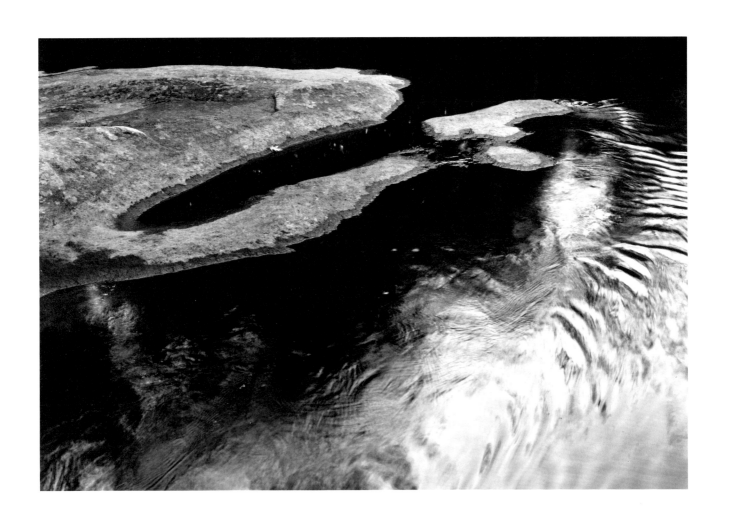

66. BLACK RIVER, COVENTRY, VERMONT, 1972

67. THINGVELLIR, ICELAND, 1974

I carry the winter photographs of my friend Fred Picker and I search for a place to be with them again. The rude colors of this California morning, cresting and surging over me, drive me to the white unfurnished room at the top of the house. I lean the photographs against the wall and sit before them on a folding chair, hands open on my knees, offering myself. I breathe and wait.

Soon it comes again, drawing me through the surface of my vision; vision as pitted and abused as the crust of an old moon by the insults daily flung at it and I am returned to that same high cool pure place within myself where these images taught me to go when I first met them. I become very still as I roam through the objects abstracted by Fred's untiring quest for significant revelation; the logic of black waters, the twisting away of a root, the silent fall of a twig at the edge of the melt, the companionship of two surviving grasses at the foot of what appears to be a global frost.

I have my sight again. My outward gaze bathed by snow, arrested by haikus of wood and weed and water is led inwards to a center as lovely as any I have known and I have a sense of soft arrival. These pictures are meditations and like other meditations they do not demand or request attention. They are unmailed invitations to be found in one's own time and way. If you stare at them they vanish; if you narrow your eyes at them, they narrow you. If you are compelled to associate, to say with your inner voice, "Oh, that looks like a face" or "Those are candy buttons," all the mysteries the pictures hold will hide behind their fan.

What you need to do, I think, is to be still and notice lightly with a wide eye and consciousness intact and with no words to say what you are seeing. As you drift from image to image, refusing to describe them to yourself, you will experience an expansion within you, a kinship with the grandeur of the cycles, a slowly growing comprehension and celebration of what is, and a sense that tragedies are as impermanent as winter when you are the cause and the effect of your own being.

When you glimpse yourself as the void through which all passes and persists, then you know, suddenly, that it is you who are the wordless universe.

Stewart Stern
March, 1979
Los Angeles

68. DOG RIVER, EAST NORTHFIELD, VERMONT, 1978

69. FIRST BRANCH, WHITE RIVER, NORTH TUNBRIDGE, VERMONT, 1978

70. FIRST BRANCH, WHITE RIVER, NORTH TUNBRIDGE, VERMONT, 1978

71. AMOS HAILE BROOK, PUTNEY, VERMONT, 1978

72. AMOS HAILE BROOK, PUTNEY, VERMONT, 1978

73. AMOS HAILE BROOK, PUTNEY, VERMONT, 1978

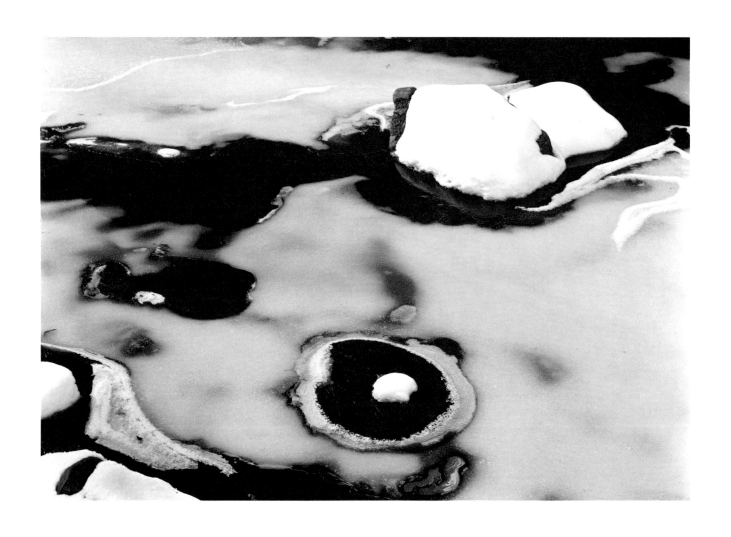

74. SECOND BRANCH, WHITE RIVER, EAST BETHEL, VERMONT, 1978

75. AMOS HAILE BROOK, PUTNEY, VERMONT, 1978

76. EAST ALSTEAD, NEW HAMPSHIRE, 1979

77. TUNBRIDGE, VERMONT, 1978

78. WESTMINSTER WEST, VERMONT, 1976

79. LOWER WATERFORD, VERMONT, 1976